Hong Kong

in pictures

Prepared by JAMES NACH

Not rice fields, but stocked fish ponds.

VISUAL
GEOGRAPHY
SERIES

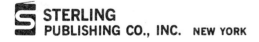

STERLING
PUBLISHING CO., INC. NEW YORK

Oak Tree Press Co., Ltd.
London & Sydney

VISUAL GEOGRAPHY SERIES

Afghanistan
Alaska
Argentina
Australia
Austria
Belgium and Luxembourg
Berlin—East and West
Bolivia
Brazil
Bulgaria
Canada
The Caribbean (English-
   Speaking Islands)
Ceylon (Sri Lanka)
Chile
China
Colombia
Costa Rica
Cuba
Czechoslovakia
Denmark
Ecuador
Egypt
El Salvador

England
Ethiopia
Fiji
Finland
France
French Canada
Ghana
Greece
Greenland
Guatemala
Haiti
Hawaii
Holland
Honduras
Hong Kong
Hungary
Iceland
India
Indonesia
Iran
Iraq
Ireland
Islands of the
   Mediterranean

Israel
Italy
Jamaica
Japan
Kenya
Korea
Kuwait
Lebanon
Liberia
Malawi
Malaysia and Singapore
Mexico
Morocco
Nepal
New Zealand
Nicaragua
Norway
Pakistan and Bangladesh
Panama and the Canal
   Zone
Peru
The Philippines
Poland
Portugal

Puerto Rico
Rhodesia
Rumania
Russia
Saudi Arabia
Scotland
Senegal
South Africa
Spain
Surinam
Sweden
Switzerland
Tahiti and the
   French Islands of
   the Pacific
Taiwan
Tanzania
Thailand
Tunisia
Turkey
Venezuela
Wales
West Germany
Yugoslavia

ACKNOWLEDGMENTS

The publishers wish to thank the British Information Services, the Hong Kong Government Information Services, the Hong Kong Tourist Association and the Hong Kong Trade Development Council for the photographs used in this book.

Revised Edition

Copyright © 1974, 1972, 1969, 1966, 1963
by Sterling Publishing Co., Inc.
419 Park Avenue South, New York, N.Y. 10016
British edition published by Oak Tree Press Co., Ltd., Nassau, Bahamas
Distributed in Australia and New Zealand by Oak Tree Press Co., Ltd.,
P.O. Box J34, Brickfield Hill, Sydney 2000, N.S.W.
Distributed in the United Kingdom and elsewhere in the British Commonwealth
by Ward Lock Ltd., 116 Baker Street, London W 1
Manufactured in the United States of America
All rights reserved
Library of Congress Catalog Card No.: 63-19163
Sterling ISBN 0-8069-1034-8 Trade   Oak Tree 7061- 6019 3
1035-6 Library

The magnificent new Ocean Terminal juts out into Hong Kong's port from the foot of Kowloon penin-sula. Hong Kong Island is in the background. The streamlined terminal has shops, restaurants, services, and entertainment as well as storage space for the large ships calling on Hong Kong, which formerly had to unload by tender.

CONTENTS

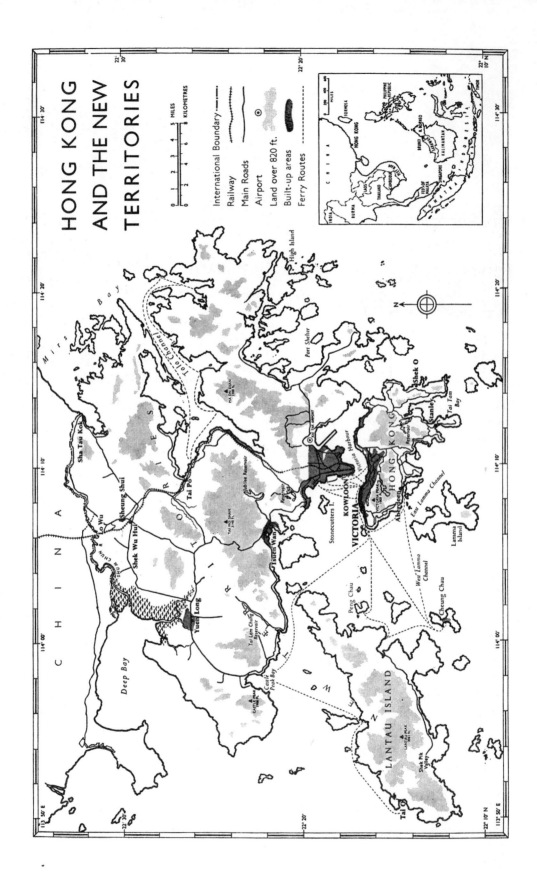

HONG KONG AND THE NEW TERRITORIES

International Boundary
Railway
Main Roads
Airport
Land over 820 ft.
Built-up areas
Ferry Routes

MILES
KILOMETRES

CHINA

Deep Bay

Mirs Bay

Sha Tau Kok

Sheung Shui

Lok Ma Chau

Shek Wu Hui

Yuen Long

Castle Peak Bay

Tai Po

Tsuen Wan

Jubilee Reservoir

Tai Lam Chung Reservoir

Tolo Channel

High Island

Port Shelter

Stonecutters I.

VICTORIA

KOWLOON

HONG KONG

Victoria Harbour

Aberdeen

Stanley

Shek O

Tai Tam Bay

Peng Chau

Cheung Chau

West Lamma Channel

East Lamma Channel

Lamma Island

LANTAU ISLAND

Shek Pik Valley

Tai O

INDEX

Beautiful gates of decorative ironwork keep unwanted visitors away from the luxurious home of a wealthy Chinese "taipan" (the local term for a business tycoon). This particular home was used during the filming of the 1957 motion picture "Soldier of Fortune."

INTRODUCTION

By modern standards of world politics Hong Kong should not exist. It is a British Crown Colony in an age when colonialism has been buried beneath the surging tides of nationalism. It is in a dangerous location, a mere appendage to Communist China, a sworn enemy of any remaining traces of Western imperialism. It has been swollen at the seams by hundreds of thousands of destitute Chinese refugees. Yet Hong Kong remains and even thrives, an amazing exception to the general rule.

Hong Kong is alive today for many reasons. British greed and Chinese obstinacy were responsible for its birth in 1841, but it took British administrative skill and commercial interests and Chinese industriousness to turn a barren island and strip of the Chinese mainland into a thriving city of millions. Recent years have not been kind to the Colony. Hong Kong had barely recovered from the ruthless Japanese military occupation during World War II when Civil War in China and subsequent Communist take-over unleashed a flood of hungry refugees on the Colony. Then the vagaries of international politics all but cut off trade with China—the Colony's lifeblood and traditional market. Hong Kong found itself locked in a desperate battle for survival.

Overnight, Hong Kong somehow transformed itself from an import-export emporium into a major industrial power of the Far East. People have proved to be the Colony's greatest resource. Chinese refugees brought with them the ingredients for success: money, skills, and the desire for hard work. People have also proved to be Hong Kong's greatest problem. Too many still live crowded into dingy tenements and ramshackle squatter villages. However, the enlightened British Colonial Administration is making a valiant effort to improve the lot of these unfortunates.

Even though Hong Kong is, as will be seen, partially owned and partially leased by Britain, it is still Chinese. Much is made of the impact of the West on Far Eastern cultures. The Chinese have accepted a great deal that the West has had to offer, but they do not forget for one moment that they are Chinese, the possessors of one of mankind's most ancient and treasured heritages. They are not about to abandon the clashing cymbals and gongs of Chinese opera for any substitute the West may offer. Exactly what the future holds in store for Hong Kong no one can be quite certain. But the Colony lives on, a sometimes harmonious sometimes strained combination of rich and poor, intrigue and industry, East and West.

(*Above*) Workers digging a well a half-century ago ran off in terror when a 20-foot geyser of crimson water erupted, without warning. The well diggers, fearing they had wounded a sacred dragon, built a temple dedicated to Kuan Yin, the Goddess of Mercy. Later, an analysis of the "bloody" water by chemists showed that deposits of mercury and sulphur were responsible. In recent years, the area has become a residential district, but the temple still remains.

(*Left*) When the British returned to Hong Kong after more than 3½ years of Japanese occupation, much of the city was in ruins. Under Japanese rule, the people of Hong Kong suffered a fate similar to those in countries overrun by Germany during World War II. Chinese guerillas operated in the New Territories throughout the war.

Daily—precisely at noon—a gun is fired in the compound of Jardine, Matheson & Company to inform residents of the Colony that it is midday. The fortune of the Company, one of the oldest and most famous British trading concerns in the Far East, was founded on the opium trade; today, however, the Company only engages in reputable enterprises. According to legend, the Port Commodore ordered the Company to fire the noonday gun as punishment for giving one of their returning officials a 21-gun salute!

HISTORY

Little more than a century ago Hong Kong was a barren island off the South China coast inhabited by a few hundred pirates and fishermen. The transformation of this inhospitable island into one of Asia's leading cities was the result of the unpleasant clash of two great civilizations—the Chinese and the Western. If it had not been for the desire of the Western nations to trade with China it is almost certain that Hong Kong would not exist today.

For ages, stories of the fabulous wealth of the Orient captured the imagination of Europe. In earlier times the Roman Empire had carried on a limited trade with the Far East. But conquests by the Moslems of the overland trade routes during the Middle Ages practically brought this commerce to a halt. However, the lure of rare gems, spices, and silks was too strong for the Europeans to remain at home. Denied access to the Far East by land, they sought new routes by sea. Portugal and Spain were the leaders.

In 1497 the Portuguese under Vasco da Gama reached India. Columbus, an Italian sailing for Spain, accidentally discovered the Americas while attempting to pioneer a new route to the East Indies. The first Portuguese reached China about 1513, and trade with the

Chinese began a few years afterwards. In 1557, Portugal established a settlement at Macao not far from the great Chinese city of Canton. (Portugal is no longer a world power but still retains Macao, which is eclipsed commercially by nearby Hong Kong and menaced politically by Communist China, as a decaying reminder of its former greatness.)

THE BRITISH ARRIVE

In the 16th century, Britain, soon to be the leading European power, failed in early efforts to trade with the Chinese. However, by 1699 the British East India Company finally succeeded in getting a share of the China trade. Dutch, French, and Spanish ships were also frequent callers at Canton. Americans began arriving in their fast clipper ships soon after the United States secured its independence.

Hong Kong may have as many as a quarter of a million narcotics users, most of them addicted to opium and heroin. Police seized this hoard of opium aboard a sampan in a typhoon shelter. Drug addiction thrives on poverty, and most victims turn to narcotics to escape the reality of their unfortunate economic situation.

The Chinese did not think well of the foreigners who came to their shores. This stemmed partly from the sometimes disgraceful conduct of the European traders and partly from the belief of the Chinese that they were

Prior to the tumultuous political events of the last decades, a traveller could board a train in Kowloon and go all the way to London, by rail, via China, Siberia, and Europe. The British section of the Kowloon-Canton Railway is only 23 miles long, but it is a vital economic link for the New Territories, and carries over six million passengers annually. The last steam engines on the line have been replaced with diesel locomotives.

The Dragon Boat Festival held in May or June commemorates a Chinese statesman who drowned himself 2,200 years ago, after the Emperor had refused to reform the corrupt Imperial Court. Rice cakes are still tossed into the water to placate the spirit of the departed official. The fierce dragon heads adorning the bows of the boats are stored in Chinese temples when the boats are not racing.

culturally superior to all other nations. In fact, the Chinese customarily referred to the Europeans as "foreign barbarians" or "red-haired devils." They had no desire to import large quantities of goods from the West, but were content to sell the Europeans tea, silk, and porcelain in return for payment in silver.

Foreigners were confined to Canton by order of the Manchu emperor. In addition, all dealings with the Chinese were handled by a small group of Chinese merchants known as the Co-hong who often made trading difficult for the Westerners. Foreigners were sometimes accused of violating unwritten laws and standards of Chinese justice, and punished accordingly. The British attempted to remedy their problems with the Chinese by diplomatic means but got nowhere. The Chinese considered the British inferior and demanded that they kowtow (bow) before the Emperor to demonstrate their "barbarian" status. Naturally, the British refused.

The issue which touched off the almost-inevitable conflict between the Chinese and the Europeans was the drug, opium. Contrary to popular belief, opium smoking did not originate in China. It was European sailors who brought

(Below) Hong Kong reluctantly operates a Berlin Wall in reverse. Because the Colony is already crammed with refugees, the Government tries to prevent any more from entering. Here, Marine Police search a junk for illegal immigrants; but many still slip in undetected. While Western statesmen applaud refugees who manage to escape from Communist China, they do not allow more than a handful to emigrate to their own countries.

The Communist Bank of China (middle left) and the British-owned Hong Kong and Shanghai Banking Corporation (middle) rise above the heart of the financial district. The Chinese bank was built slightly taller than the adjacent British bank for prestige purposes, but a second British bank has eclipsed both of its predecessors in height.

Private cars and buses are seen arriving on Hong Kong Island after driving through the new Cross Harbour Tunnel which connects the island with the mainland.

the evil habit with them to China some time during the 17th century. Unfortunately for China, opium addiction spread rapidly throughout the country and the demand for the drug increased. Chinese government efforts to stop the opium trade were futile, for the Europeans, interested in selling opium, went to great lengths, including bribery and smuggling. By the 1830's, trade was brisk and a fortune in opium was being smuggled into China annually. The British were the chief offenders since they controlled India, the main source of opium supply. Not a few great fortunes were founded upon profits from the opium trade.

The Chinese became desperate, for the flood of opium was not only corrupting the population, but also draining precious silver from the country to pay the Europeans for the drug. A special commissioner, Lin Tse-hsü, was dispatched to Canton in 1839 to wipe out the opium trade once and for all. He took drastic action. Western trading establishments were surrounded and the Europeans were forced to surrender their huge stocks of opium to the Chinese for immediate destruction. Lin also demanded that all foreigners promise never again to import opium, upon pain of death. The British refused to sign the promise and

departed for Macao. However, the Portuguese were not very happy to have the British opium agents as guests and suggested that it might be wise for them to leave. The British then moved on to Hong Kong. Hostilities followed soon afterwards.

The Opium War, sometimes more politely termed the First Anglo-Chinese War, was a one-sided affair; for the Chinese at first failed to realize that they had taken on the world's leading nation. The British took formal possession of Hong Kong in January, 1841, as the result of a preliminary treaty. However, the Chinese Government objected to giving away so much—while the British demanded still more. In fact, Elliot, the British representative, was recalled to London for being willing to settle for such a worthless piece of real estate as Hong Kong Island.

A series of successful British naval raids along the South China coast finally forced the Chinese to accept a humiliating settlement. Among other things, Britain received Hong Kong Island and collected a large indemnity from China. The Co-hong was ended and five Chinese ports were opened to British commerce. Not a word was said about abolishing the opium trade.

Two dragon boats race towards the finish line. Coxswains urge their crews on by beating out fast rhythms on drums. The boats are usually between 80 and 100 feet long, and are manned by younger members of the Chinese trade guilds and associations.

The new Colony at Hong Kong did not get off to a good start. Fires and typhoons destroyed large areas of the infant settlement and malaria epidemics killed hundreds. Many residents fled to Macao to save themselves. In Britain, a popular insult of the times was to tell someone to "Go to Hong Kong."

A FREE PORT

But the British laid the seeds for Hong Kong's future prosperity. Instead of making the island an exclusive commercial preserve for themselves, the British declared Hong Kong a free port. People from all nations were welcomed and no duties were levied on imports and exports. Traders from all parts of the world found it safe, cheap, and convenient to ship their goods to Hong Kong for subsequent distribution throughout southern China. Similarly, Hong Kong served as a collection point for Chinese exports.

Population pressures in China made Hong Kong a leading embarkation port for thousands of Chinese seeking a better life elsewhere. At first, most of the emigrants went to Southeast Asia, but the discovery of gold in California and later in Australia attracted many Chinese. The difficult western portion of the first transcontinental railway across the United States was built almost entirely by Chinese workers. Unfortunately, many of the Chinese emigrants were subjected by profit-hungry ship captains to conditions not very different from the infamous African slave trade. Britain, alone among the Western powers, took pains to make sure the departing Chinese were treated decently.

During the 1850's and 1860's, many Chinese fled to Hong Kong to escape the ravages of a bitter rebellion then raging in China. Twenty years after its founding, the colony had a population of over 120,000. Since that time refugees have continued to flock to Hong Kong, peaceful under British protection, whenever unrest or wars upset China. Sun Yat-sen, leader of the Revolution of 1911 that overthrew the Manchus and established a republic in China, often marveled at Britain's ability to maintain calm in Hong Kong in the midst of so

much disturbance. Sun Yat-sen was in a good position to know, for he spent several years in Hong Kong as a student and was a frequent visitor while plotting the downfall of the Manchu dynasty.

A second war between China and the European powers broke out in 1856 and continued until 1860. China was decisively defeated, and once again was forced to sign a disadvantageous treaty with the Western nations which opened more of the country to the "barbarian" traders. Britain also received the Kowloon Peninsula opposite Hong Kong Island. The opium trade was made legal. In 1898, Britain leased a large tract of the mainland north of Kowloon from the Chinese government for a period of 99 years. This was the last addition to the Colony.

The Chinese and Europeans each kept to themselves. The Chinese preferred to follow their time-honored traditions and occupations and leave international trade and administration of the Colony in the hands of the British. Nor was there much in the way of informal social exchange between the two groups. However, the British took some pains to protect Chinese interests. An 1865 ruling guaranteed equality under law to all residents irrespective of race. The post of Secretary for Chinese Affairs was created to protect the interests of the Chinese community. It was only when Chinese began receiving Western education and training that they started to take an active share in Hong Kong's commerce and government. The first Chinese member of the Legislative Council was appointed in 1880.

OVERCROWDING

Hong Kong has had to face the problems of all large cities, but to a more acute degree than most. Unsanitary living conditions brought on by overcrowding have always been a primary concern. Until well into the 20th century, the bulk of the Chinese population remained suspicious of British attempts to introduce Western sanitation procedures into their way of life. The black plague, which frequently killed off great portions of the population of Europe during the Middle Ages, broke out at Hong

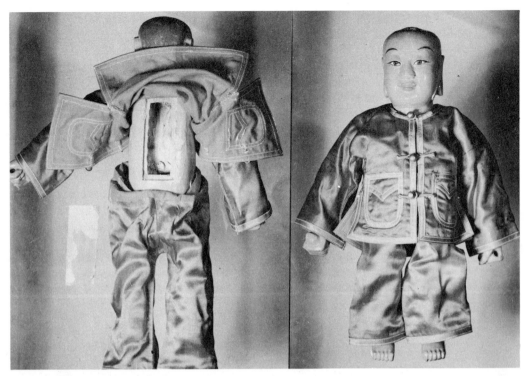

An innocent-looking child's doll can become an insidious tool in the hands of a narcotics smuggler. Heroin was hidden in the hollow cavity in the back of this doll. Because of its excellent transportation connections with the rest of the world, Hong Kong serves as an unwilling collection and distribution point of narcotics. International crime syndicates smuggle opium into the Colony from the areas in Southeast Asia where it is grown and transform it into its more deadly derivatives, morphine and heroin, which are then exported to their criminal brothers in Europe and America. Despite their efforts, Colony police are only able to halt a small fraction of the total narcotics flow.

Kong in 1894. During this epidemic, two visiting Japanese doctors made the important discovery that the plague is spread by rats. Thereafter, strenuous efforts were made to exterminate the Colony's rodent population.

Although Hong Kong is a British colony, it is physically part of China and most of its inhabitants are still Chinese. Important events in China are bound to have some effect in or on Hong Kong. This has been particularly true since the turn of the century. The Revolution of 1911 engineered by Sun Yat-sen awakened Chinese nationalism. The 75 years of selfish exploitation and unfair humiliation at the hands of the Western powers were too much for the proud Chinese spirit to bear. During the 1920's, the Chinese began fighting back against the foreign interests. British goods

were boycotted. British subjects received the largest share of attention from the angry Chinese because Britain was, at the time, the leading Western power in the Far East. In Hong Kong, there were several large strikes by trade unions.

The activities of China's ancient foe, Japan, diverted Chinese attention from the West. The Japanese seized Manchuria in 1931, and in 1937 invaded the remainder of China. Canton was captured in 1938, cutting off Hong Kong from what was left of free China. A torrent of over 750,000 refugees swelled the population of the Colony to 1,600,000.

Japan attacked Hong Kong on the same day surprise raids were launched on Pearl Harbor and British Malaya. The Colony was in no position to withstand the powerful Japanese assault, so it surrendered on December 25, 1941, after bitter fighting. The following 3½ years of Japanese occupation were not pleasant. Trade and commerce ground to a halt, and food was in short supply. Over one million Chinese had left the Colony by the end of World War II.

Hong Kong recovered rapidly after the War, but the struggle for control of China between Chiang Kai-shek's Nationalists and Mao Tse-tung's Communists started a greater flood of refugees than the Colony had ever seen. They came from all levels of society: peasants, intellectuals, criminals, and businessmen alike. In 1945, Hong Kong had 1,600,000 residents. Five years later the total was 2,360,000. There was simply no room to house and insufficient food to feed the newcomers. Hundreds of thousands were forced to sleep in the streets or live in unhealthy squatter huts built of wooden

crates and tin cans. To cope with the problem, the Colony's government has undertaken massive programs of low-cost public housing, school and hospital construction, and other desperately-needed social services. Government encouragement of private industry has helped create thousands of new jobs. However, the struggle against poverty is really just beginning, and it will take a heroic effort on the part of both the British and the Chinese if the battle is to be won.

In 1967 large-scale demonstrations against British rule were staged by Communist groups within the Colony, making the future more uncertain than ever.

Late in 1971, Communist China was admitted to the United Nations. It remained to be seen what effect this would have on Hong Kong.

Walled villages in the New Territories are reminders of the lawless years during the 17th century, before the Manchu dynasty had consolidated its control over southern China. Danger from marauding bandit gangs has vanished and villagers have now built windows into formerly solid walls. Ducks and lotuses are raised in the moat.

The combination of rice fields, picturesque bridges, and rugged hills gives the New Territories a charm of their own. One would hardly guess that the bustle and congestion of the city are only a few miles away from this pleasant spot.

THE LAND

Hong Kong is located on China's southeast coast near the mouth of the Pearl River. Portuguese Macao is 40 miles to the west, and Canton, site of the first contacts between Europeans and Chinese, is only 90 miles to the northwest.

The Colony resembles a spattered ink blot. The New Territories and adjacent islands, leased from China for 99 years from 1898, form by far the largest portion of the Colony's land area, some 365 square miles all told. Kowloon and Hong Kong Island, owned in perpetuity by Great Britain, have a total area of only 33 square miles.

Hong Kong's entire coastline is jagged and broken, providing many deep, sheltered bays and coves for shipping. Victoria Harbour, about which the Colony's commercial life is focused, is considered one of the world's best natural ports. However, the more than 240 islands and islets of various shapes and sizes in nearby waters make navigation a bit tricky for the novice. There is little flat land in Hong Kong. In most parts of the Colony, barren granite mountains rise abruptly from the sea. Tai Mo Shan in the New Territories is the highest peak with an elevation of 3,140 feet; although, Victoria Peak towering over the

An FM radio transmitter has been installed on Hong Kong Island to provide static-free broadcasting to all the Colony's residents, whether they live in urban areas or remote, mountain-rimmed valleys. Government and commercial radio stations provide both Chinese and English services. A commercial closed-circuit television network also operates. The long, thin strip of land jutting into the Harbour is the runway of Kai Tak Airport. Part of the Kowloon Peninsula can be seen to the left of the landward end of the runway.

(Below) Rice fields seen from the air form a delicate mosaic. Piles of harvested rice dot many of the fields.

Harbour is a much more familiar landmark for residents and tourists.

Building space has been in short supply and high demand as a result of the mountainous terrain, but Hong Kong has developed an ingenious solution for the problem. For quite some time the Colony has been growing in a very literal sense. When new land is needed, rock is taken from the mountains and dumped into the sea. Thousands of homes, factories, and commercial establishments stand on re-claimed land, and many new acres are added every year.

CLIMATE

Hong Kong lies just below the tropic of Cancer so one can officially classify it as being in the tropics. However, the Colony's weather is controlled by the monsoons, the seasonal prevailing winds which determine the climates of many Asian countries. From October to April, the cool, dry winds flow down from the northeast. Clear skies and moderate temperatures make the months from October to December the most pleasant for tourist visits.

Blocks of apartment buildings and offices cling to the steep slopes of Victoria Peak, which rises abruptly above the narrow strip of flat land along the waterfront.

Century Tower, containing luxurious apartments is a new landmark on Hong Kong Island.

Temperatures are usually in the 70's at this time of year. February is the coldest month with temperatures dropping down to the 40's and 50's. About May, the northeast monsoon dies away and winds shift, coming from the southwest. This is the beginning of the rainy season, a period of hot, humid days with frequent showers. Temperatures often rise into the 80's and 90's, and most of Hong Kong's normal precipitation of about 85 inches falls between May and September. (New York City has about half as much rain spread evenly throughout the year.)

(Below) Old buildings are falling under the weight of the wrecker's ball to provide room for new construction in the crowded business district. The grounds of the Hong Kong Cricket Club (lower right) remain sacred. A new, modern-looking city hall on the sea front is part of a sorely-needed civic development plan. Included are Hong Kong's first public library, an art gallery, museum and concert hall. Ferries shuttle back and forth between Hong Kong Island and Kowloon, among the scores of ships anchored in the Harbour.

(*Above*) *Just about anything one could desire can be purchased at an open-air street market. Babies often travel to market strapped to their mothers' backs. At night, gasoline lanterns illuminate the scene.*

Since its founding, Hong Kong has been plagued by a shortage of fresh water. Population growth has all but nullified the gains in water supply from construction of the Tai Lam Chung reservoir, and others like it. The Colony now augments its own supply with water purchased from Communist China.

(Above) A plane has just touched down at Kai Tak Airport. Because no suitable site for a jet-age airfield could be found in the Colony, the Hong Kong Government built one from scratch by constructing a 1½-mile-long promontory jutting into Kowloon Bay. Nineteen international airlines provide frequent service to destinations in all parts of the world. Large annual increases in tourist arrivals, plus the advent of "jumbo" jets, will soon make Kai Tak inadequate, however.

The Star Ferry, running between Kowloon and Hong Kong Island, covers the one-mile distance in about 7 minutes. When the first-class fare was raised one penny, riots occurred. A new 1-1/8th-mile Cross-Harbour Tunnel was completed in 1972 with 4 traffic lanes capable of handling 60,000 vehicles each day.

Statue Square and the City Hall are in the heart of Victoria. In the background is Kowloon.

Quite often Hong Kong receives unwanted visitors. These are typhoons, the name given to hurricanes in the Pacific Ocean area. Because it is located on the coast, Hong Kong frequently suffers the full force of these storms. Winds, sometimes exceeding 100 miles per hour, can cause incredible damage in a few hours. Roofs are torn off, fishermen drowned, and oyster beds destroyed; everyone suffers at least to some degree, and millions are lost in property values.

The Peak Tramway has hauled millions of passengers 1,300 feet up Victoria Peak since the track was opened in 1888. Tourists ride the Tram to enjoy the spectacular view of the Colony it affords, while many residents of the Peak use it to commute to the city for business and shopping. Tram cars are pulled up the mountain by steel cables attached to electric motors.

This overflow tunnel for the new Shek Pik Reservoir on Lantau Island may not see much use since domestic and industrial demand for fresh water runs far ahead of supply. Since no major river passes through the Colony, Hong Kong must depend entirely on local rainfall to replenish its reservoirs. A severe drought during the spring of 1963—the worst since 1929, when water had to be imported by boat from Shanghai—virtually dried up all reservoirs and caused strict water rationing.

WILDLIFE AND VEGETATION

Despite the great population of Hong Kong Island, a unique form of wildlife remains. This is the barking deer, an animal resembling a dog in size and bark, but having the antlers of a deer. It lives in the highlands of the Island and emits its bark as it prowls during the night hours. Several large members of the cat family occasionally cross into the New Territories from China. Tigers have not been seen for some time, but a leopard killed a large amount of farmers' livestock during 1957. Many snakes including the king cobra live in Hong Kong, but they rarely harm anyone since most of them are not poisonous. Also found in the Colony is the atlas moth, the world's largest, with a wing-span of up to nine inches.

Hong Kong does not have many large forested areas, especially since the Japanese occupation, when the hard-pressed residents were forced to cut down most of the Colony's trees for fuel. However, the Hong Kong Government is undertaking extensive reforestation, and thousands of seedling trees are planted annually. Schoolchildren are sometimes invited to participate, so that they may learn the importance of forests to the community. Hong Kong's landscape is brightened by a large variety of flowering shrubs renowned for their lush blossoms.

(Right) The Shatin Valley is one of the few level areas in the New Territories. All available land is subdivided into innumerable rice paddies, with the dark forms of trees marking villages and farmhouses. Rice grown in the Shatin Valley is of such high quality that at one time it was sent to Peking to satisfy the delicate appetite of the Emperor and his court.

(*Left*) *The sight of new construction encased in bamboo scaffolding often sends shivers down the spines of first-time visitors to Hong Kong. Accidents are infrequent, however, and lashed bamboo poles have proven to be as effective as steel scaffolding. Because steel girders are very expensive, most new structures in Hong Kong, are built of steel-reinforced concrete.*

(*Right*) *Double decker buses cruise up and down Nathan Road. Cars of various national origins crowd the streets, causing traffic headaches for pedestrians and Government planners alike—just as in any large city.*

Hong Kong is one of the most competitive markets in the world. Its busy commercial life is reflected in this street in the Mongkok District of Kowloon.

The visit of Princess Margaret to Hong Kong in 1966 was of great social and economic significance to the Colony.

Welfare organizations care for Hong Kong's destitute, blind and otherwise handicapped residents who are unable to provide for themselves. As a result, there are fewer beggars in Hong Kong than in other Asian lands. Chinese Kaifongs (voluntary community welfare associations) undertake many worthy projects of this type.

Accommodations in resettlement blocks are simple, but far better than the substandard conditions in which refugees previously lived. A single communal bathroom serves an entire floor, and electricity is provided only for those willing to pay extra for it. This family pays less rent for their new flat than they did formerly for an unhealthy tenement cubicle.

Crowded, unhealthy tenements make tuberculosis a major killer in Hong Kong. Government campaigns, prompt BCG vaccination of new-born children, and the work of the Hong Kong Anti-Tuberculosis Association have slashed the death rate from tuberculosis by more than two-thirds, however, in only ten years. All 544 beds of the Grantham Hospital are used for treatment of tuberculosis sufferers. The building was constructed in the form of a thin vertical slab to allow fresh air to circulate freely.

GOVERNMENT

Because it is a Crown Colony, Hong Kong is not self-governing. The Governor is the most important official in the Colony, and he is appointed by the British Government which has a long tradition of appointing capable men to important posts in its colonial dependencies.

Democratic government does not exist in Hong Kong, but this does not mean that the residents of the Colony are suffering under the harsh rule of an autocratic régime. Hong Kong's Government falls under the watchful eye of Britain's Secretary of State for the Colonies.

Furthermore, two Councils, the Executive and the Legislative, advise the Governor on important matters. If the Governor acts contrary to the advice given by the Executive Council he must explain to the British Government why he did so. Special laws for Hong Kong are made by the Governor with the advice and consent of the Legislative Council. This Council also regulates the Colony's finances.

Members of the Executive and Legislative Councils are not elected by the people of Hong Kong. Some, such as the Secretary for Chinese

Until a disastrous 1954 squatter fire left 53,000 people homeless, the Hong Kong Government took little interest in the plight of refugees. The fire caused a complete about-face in Government policy and tall resettlement blocks began mushrooming all over the colony.

Affairs, are automatically members by virtue of their positions in the Colony's administration. Others, known as "unofficial" members, are nominated for their posts by the Governor, in most cases, or by the Chamber of Commerce and the Justices of the Peace. Most members are British or Chinese; however, the Portuguese and Indian communities usually have representation in the Councils.

Formerly, almost all important positions in Government were filled by Britons. But now a new era is at hand. Residents of the Colony, mostly Chinese of course, are being encouraged and trained to occupy administrative and professional positions in the Government. At present over 40 per cent of these posts are held by local people and the percentage increases annually. The Hong Kong Government is investing large amounts of money to see that they receive proper training for their jobs, and many candidates are sent overseas for special training not available in the Colony.

POLITICS

Anyone born in Hong Kong is considered a British subject. However, there are very few among the Chinese segment of the population who consider themselves British subjects, only some lawyers, civil servants, and others associated either with Government or Western commerce. Most Chinese think of themselves as Chinese and not as subjects of a foreign Queen whom they know only from pictures. But neither is there a sense of local nationalism in Hong Kong likely to spark a desire for independence. The only nationalists present are the pro-Chinese.

Shoulder poles have been used to transport burdens from before the beginning of recorded Chinese history. Hakka women, wearing traditional cloth-draped straw hats, are carrying stones for use in a village self-help project. The Hong Kong Government supplies money and technical assistance and villagers supply the necessary muscle power to carry out road-building, irrigation, and other community-improvement projects.

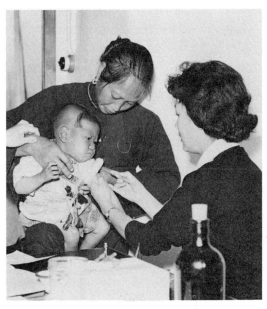

Formerly, patients had to go to the clinic; now the clinic comes to the patients. Motor launches converted into floating clinics by the Hong Kong Jockey Club and donated to the Government make scheduled stops in various remote reaches of the New Territories. The parents of this baby would not have made the long trip to a mainland clinic to have their child vaccinated.

Wanchai's waterfront has a new look. The modern complex of flyovers (cloverleafs) has largely been built on land reclaimed from the sea.

All types of political opinion have their adherents among Hong Kong's Chinese. Some are supporters of Mao Tse-tung's (Communist) People's Republic of China; others are followers of Chiang Kai-shek's Taiwan (Formosa) régime, the Republic of China. Many refrain from giving their allegiance to either side, but are waiting to see who triumphs. Since there is no democratic government in the Colony, political parties have not developed. But political ideologies have a way of working themselves into everyday life. Hong Kong's trade unions are divided into two rival groups. As expected, one federation of unions supports Communist China and the other the Taiwan Nationalists. A wider range of political opinion can be found in the Colony's 30-odd major newspapers, three of which are in English.

Hong Kong has been successful because it has been able to offer security and rule by law to all who have come. It is a safe place to do business. Until the recent overcrowding caused by the influx of refugees, the British welcomed to Hong Kong anyone willing to keep the peace, no matter what his political views. The majesty of British law, represented by the bewigged judges of the various local courts, has to be upheld at all costs; otherwise, the Colony's reputation as a safe place for trade and industry in the midst of frequent Asian turmoil will be jeopardized, and Hong Kong's prosperity will vanish.

In an effort to increase its water storage capacity, Hong Kong is constructing a dam 1½ miles long across the Plover Cove inlet, thus creating a reserve of 30,000,000,000 gallons in an artificial fresh-water lake. The project is to be completed by 1978.

Some Chinese prefer to wear Western-style business suits; others dress in traditional Chinese garb. There are still several hundred rickshaws operating in the Colony, one of the last places in the world they can be found. The Communists allowed them soon after they came into power in China. Many people consider it degrading for one man to pull another.

THE PEOPLE

To call Hong Kong Chinese is something of an understatement—an overwhelming 99 per cent of the population is Chinese.

The 1961 census, the first taken in 30 years, fixed the Colony's population at 3,133,131. Most of the people are concentrated in a densely-packed urban area. About four-fifths of the population is jammed into 10 square miles of land, chiefly the narrow strip of comparatively flat terrain along the north shore of Hong Kong Island and the Kowloon Peninsula. About 500,000 people live in the New Territories, and over 150,000 make their homes on boats in the Colony's waters. The population of Hong Kong is growing at a fantastic rate. In the four years from 1961-65 the population increased by nearly 25 per cent to over 3,800,000. In 1973, the population estimate was 4,200,000.

Asian lands, especially China and India, are often noted for their rapidly-increasing popu-

Low-rent housing in Hong Kong. This shows a section of one of the blocks recently occupied at So Uk Estate. Each flat, in addition to the connecting balconies, has its own verandah.

Nathan Road in Kowloon is Hong Kong's version of the Great White Way. A wide variety of merchandise attracts crowds of shoppers to the stores, which usually remain open until ten or eleven in the evening.

lations. Hong Kong is no exception to this pattern. In a few years the population may pass the 5,000,000 mark, even without a sizeable influx of refugees. Only energetic Government action in expanding social services, together with some growth in manufacturing, can prevent the Colony from being literally overwhelmed by people.

For most refugees, Hong Kong is the last stop. Few countries in the world will admit more than a handful of Chinese immigrants. A few refugees are lucky enough to have relatives living in the United States who can help them begin life afresh in the New World. A scattering of others manage to emigrate to Britain (for employment by other Chinese), or to some of the underdeveloped nations where populations are sparse and the demand for technical skills great. But the vast majority of Chinese refugees in Hong Kong must remain where they are.

The largest segment of Hong Kong's Chinese population consists of Cantonese from China's Kwangtung Province which adjoins the Colony. In the New Territories, there are large numbers of other Chinese groups, chiefly the Hakka, Hoklo, and Tanka. The Hakka have been farmers in the New Territories for many centuries, but the more-powerful Cantonese often forced the Hakka to take undesirable land while they seized the best farming areas for themselves. The Tanka and Hoklo are the boat people, who spend their lives on junks and other craft in and about the Colony. In addition, there are smaller groups of Chinese from Shanghai, Peking, and other faraway parts of China.

Although overshadowed by the vast numbers of Chinese, the members of the various minority groups play an important part in the Colony's life. Men from the four corners of the earth live in Hong Kong. They are attracted to the Colony for a variety of reasons. Britons are there as businessmen, bankers, and Govern-

33

Even the poorest Chinese pay careful attention to their diets. For a few pennies one can order a delicious meal of chopped roast pork and noodles, or any custom-cooked variation, from a roadside food stall. Customers often prefer to squat, rather than sit, while eating.

The age of cellophane-wrapped meat and fish has not yet come to Hong Kong. Chinese housewives demand fresh food, and fish for this market arrive very much alive, swimming about in tanks of water.

Hard bargaining can often reduce prices at food stalls. The proprietress is cutting sugar cane stalks into more conveniently-sized lengths, while a customer makes her selection.

Illiterate residents hire the services of a letter writer when they wish to correspond with someone. As a sideline, this letter writer prepares goodluck scrolls on brilliant red paper. They can be seen hanging on the wall above his desk.

(Below) Street "libraries" stocked with Chinese comic books provide diversion for Hong Kong youngsters with nothing better to do. The owner of this stand charges a small rental fee for the "privilege" of reading volumes from his collection.

Newspapers are popular in Hong Kong, as they are everywhere. More than a score of Chinese dailies vie with one another for circulation. Chinese magazines, featuring the familiar assortment of motion-picture stars, babies, and comic-book heroes, are draped over the front of the stand. The young girl is pushing rice into her mouth with chopsticks.

ment officers. Americans are there to watch over assorted commercial interests. A number of other Americans are employed as officials and clerks at the large United States Consulate, presumably to watch over China since America does not have diplomatic relations with the Communist state. Communities of Portuguese, Jews and Indians—Moslems, Sikhs, Parsees and Hindus—have lived in the Colony almost from the time of its founding in 1841.

Some men come to Hong Kong to escape a criminal past. Others are political refugees, victims of World War II or revolutions in distant lands. The presence of Poles, Hungarians, White Russians, and other Eastern Europeans testifies to recent political upheavals in their countries. Talk of counter-revolution and sabotage is common among such groups, but the British are not particularly concerned as long as this talk does not threaten the security of Hong Kong. Other stateless persons—truly men without a country—come from a multitude

of fascinating backgrounds. Some are considered undesirable and the British are pleased when they leave the Colony. Not long ago, one such individual boarded a ferry for Portuguese Macao. Unfortunately, the Portuguese wanted no part of him and promptly placed him on the return boat to Hong Kong. However, the British did not want him back, and he soon found himself bouncing between Hong Kong and Macao like a tennis ball. After world-wide publicity and several months of enforced ferry riding, he was finally able to gain entry into another country.

CHINESE LIFE IN HONG KONG

Hong Kong is truly a place where East really meets West. But such a general description is only partially correct. While the Colony's Chinese population has been willing to adopt hundreds of things from the West, the Chinese

(Left) Sons traditionally follow in the footsteps of their fishermen fathers, among Hong Kong's boat dwellers. Schools and hospitals have helped reduce illiteracy and disease, but despite land attractions, the boat people stubbornly cling to their floating homes.

Chinese New Year occurs annually during January or February, depending on the intricate workings of the Chinese lunar calendar. Workers receive bonuses from their employers, and debts and grievances are cleared. Families celebrate by visiting relatives and exchanging gifts. A deafening barrage of firecrackers echoes through the streets of the city for two whole days, supposedly for the purpose of driving away evil spirits. Often, firecrackers are exploded in chains hung from the upper storeys of buildings, creating awesome piles of debris for street cleaners.

Like the floating clinics, the flying doctor service brings modern medicine to inaccessible New Territories villages. The doctor and his assistants will treat minor ills of the villagers and vaccinate the children.

remain very much Chinese. The contributions of the West are like frosting on the great cake of Chinese culture, which reaches several thousand years back into antiquity.

The Chinese are intensely proud of their heritage from the past, and with good reason. At the time when most of Europe was inhabited by tribes of savage warriors garbed in animal skins, and the New World was as yet undiscovered, China had developed a highly-refined civilization of its own. The Chinese had invented gunpowder and movable type long before these two influential discoveries made their appearance in Europe. Confucius, Mencius, and Lao Tzu, China's best-known philosophers, preceded many Western philosophers.

But over the ages China's society had become a closed culture. Anyone willing to accept the Chinese way of life was welcome, but the thought of their learning anything from foreign "barbarians" never occurred to the Chinese. However, the 1839 war with Britain and succeeding disastrous defeats at the hands of the Western powers taught China the bitter lesson that the West was better armed and more powerful in a military sense.

(Below) A 165-foot pagoda crowns the Tiger Balm Gardens, built by a Chinese millionaire—the late Aw Boon Haw—who made his fortune selling Tiger Balm, an alleged cure-all. Garish statues of painted wood and concrete depict scenes from Chinese mythology.

Not too many people arrive at the floating clinics in wooden tubs, but these youngsters made it there and back, enjoying every moment of their trip!

(Below) It's no secret who has died; his picture and name are prominently displayed atop the hearse. Survivors of the deceased will give a funeral feast later, for the mourners.

(Above) White, not black, is the traditional Chinese mourning dress. Processions sometimes a mile long follow the coffin through city streets to the cemetery. Brass bands are usually a part of the procession, and professional mourners dressed in sackcloth are hired to wail for the deceased.

The disastrous flood of 1966 washed buildings down the steep hillsides, wrecked cars and left a residue of mud blocking streets on Hong Kong Island.

At the same time there was a growing awareness that Western culture and technology was not all "barbarian"; in fact, it was quite a useful thing to have. More recently, a major problem for the Chinese has been to try to decide just how much to accept from Europe, America, and other areas. The present rulers of mainland China have over-enthusiastically accepted one pattern of European thought—communism. Mao Tse-tung and other leaders of Communist China have sought to alter age-old Chinese customs radically: Confucianism, arranged marriages, the traditional family structure, and scores of other features of Chinese life. All these have been consigned to the trash heap by the Communist régime. While some of these changes have undoubtedly been beneficial for the operation of the state, many of them have not been popular. The shock of this ruthless transformation has in many ways been painful for the Chinese living on the mainland.

In Hong Kong, Western culture and technology—democratic or communistic—have not been forced upon the Chinese living there. But the Chinese are an alert people. Shaken from a dangerous national pride by a century of European imperialism, they have eagerly adopted many valuable and useful things from the West. Naturally, some of the less enviable aspects of Western culture have also entered Chinese life, but this was inevitable. The most important lesson to remember is that the

Chinese in Hong Kong and elsewhere, living outside of Communist China, have not at all rejected their traditional culture. Much has been taken from the West, and Chinese life has in some ways been changed by its contact with Western life; but basically the Chinese remain very much the Chinese they always were.

The family has always been a major cornerstone of Chinese life. A Chinese family is much larger than its counterpart in the West, for it includes grandparents, uncles, aunts, and other relatives. Traditionally, the oldest male is leader of the family and all others owe obedience to him. According to Chinese ethics, younger members of the family must respect their elders. A son must respect the decisions and commands of his father, a younger brother must respect those of an elder brother, and a wife those of her husband.

Families operate on the principle of united action. Although there are almost certainly bound to be differences among the members of such an extended group, the family must present a single front to the rest of the world. In the past, the entire family was blamed for the irresponsible actions of one of its members. This conflicts with a basic tenet of Anglo-American justice which holds the individual, rather than the family, responsible for his actions. In Hong Kong, and also in China itself, justice is administered along Western

41

A young lad from a squatter village surveys the tragic aftermath of a fire which destroyed his home and all the possessions of his family. 50,000 persons were left homeless by this fire.

lines. But there are many matters of everyday life that never reach the courts of law; to a certain degree the family still retains control over these actions of its members.

Even greater in extent than the family is the clan, which is composed of many families having the same surname and able to trace descent to a common male ancestor. The clan functions as a kind of private social welfare organization, regulating its members and providing them with assistance in times of need. But, because of the impact of Western culture (which encourages the development of the individual rather than of the group), and because of the chaos resulting from the arrival of hundreds of thousands of refugees from China, the clan no longer has the same strength it formerly had. However, in the rural areas of the New Territories where the population is more stable and farther away from immediate contact with Western culture, the traditional values of Chinese life are much more in evidence.

Formerly, all Chinese marriages were arranged by the parents of the bride and groom. The parents of the groom would conduct discreet inquiries about the locality until they found a girl whom they thought worthy of entering their family. A middleman usually served as an intermediary between the families. If the parents of the girl agreed, the wedding was planned, usually on a day picked by a fortune-teller. The actual wedding ceremony, when bride and groom met each other for the first time, was elaborate. The bride would arrive at her new home in a sedan chair draped with red silk. She then had to pay homage to her husband and to her husband's ancestors. As with so many other things today in Hong

Government and private relief agencies pitch in to help victims of squatter fires. The vast but orderly sea of people queuing up for food gives some idea of the cost of such a fire in terms of human misery.

Kong, Chinese marriage customs are also changing. More and more young men and women choose for themselves the mate they are going to marry, rather than leaving the choice to their parents. Modern couples usually dispense with much of the ancient wedding ritual. White wedding gowns and Western-style suits are fast replacing the traditional robes and gowns of old China.

The Chinese like to raise large families. Whereas two or three children are the average in Western families, Chinese families often have six or eight. Male children have always been held more desirable than females, and a major duty of every Chinese wife is to provide the family with a son to carry on the family name. The birth of a first son is an occasion for great rejoicing. However, the position of women in Chinese society is becoming more equal to that of men, as it is almost everywhere else in the world. Women in Hong Kong now work alongside men in schools, factories, offices, and laboratories.

People of the Far East, including the Chinese, are often ignorantly accused of pre-occupying themselves with "saving face." Actually, "face" is just as important in the West as it is in the East. A government official in Europe or America may be removed from his job by a superior, but he is usually granted the privilege of being allowed to resign "for reasons of health" or a similar, innocent-sounding cause. Everyone knows that he has been dismissed from office, but by "resigning" he has saved his "face." Because the Chinese are so adept at techniques of face-saving, Westerners sometimes become unfairly convinced that it is an exclusive trait of the Orient.

Because of the impact on the West on Chinese culture some people are convinced that it is just a matter of time before the Chinese become completely Westernized. This is very unlikely. The great problem for the Chinese of Hong Kong and elsewhere is to be able to absorb what is best from the West, while retaining the best features of their own culture. There is no reason at all why the Chinese should have to surrender their time-tested traditions of scholarship, literature,

Soldiers from the British Army dole out rations of rice, vegetables and meat to fire victims.

religion, art, and music to "upstart" Western influences.

RELIGION

Three great and ancient religions have influenced the Chinese. Two of these, Confucianism and Taoism, originated in China while the third, Buddhism, came to China from India. Unlike the West, where a religious person considers himself a Protestant, Catholic, or Jew, a Chinese usually does not think of himself as belonging to one religion any more than to another.

Confucianism and Taoism are not strictly religions but philosophies. The teachings of Confucius, a scholar, teacher, and government official of the sixth and fifth centuries B.C., were aimed at producing an ideal society: virtue, righteousness and moderation among the princes and government officials were essential, for it would inspire the remainder of the people to act properly. Confucius urged the continuance of ancestor worship and other ancient rituals to bind the society together. Attempts have been made to turn Confucianism into a religion, but were only partly successful because the common man felt little kinship

Offerings of oranges and other foods are often placed before the altars of Chinese temples by the faithful. Burning incense gives temple interiors a pungent aroma.

with a philosophy which appealed mainly to intellectuals. Confucius was and still is regarded as a great sage, but not as a god or religious figure.

Taoism, as originally preached, taught that happiness can be had only by conforming to nature—the Tao or controlling principle of the universe. Taoists valued the simple life and shunned the elaborate ethics and concern with government that occupied the Confucian scholars. Taoism also offered the promise of immortality to the faithful. Gradually, however, Taoism became mixed with popular folk religion, and alchemy, witchcraft, and astrology all entered into its ritual.

Buddhism, an import from India, also offered salvation. The type of Buddhism popular in China was the Mahayana school as distinguished from the Hinayana Buddhism of Southeast Asia. The Mahayana Buddhist monk sought salvation for everyone and put off his own salvation to help others towards the goal. Popular heavens and hells soon entered Chinese Buddhism as did many gods, the best known being Kwan Yin, the goddess of mercy.

The rulers of Communist China are trying their best to eliminate religion from Chinese life. All three of the major religions have more or less withered away under pressure from the government. But in Hong Kong religion survives, although in a weakened condition, mostly because of a lack of religious zeal among the Chinese. There are several Buddhist monasteries scattered about the Colony, chiefly in picturesque rural locations in the New Territories. Buddhist and Taoist temples can be found throughout Hong Kong, usually dedicated to a particular god or goddess. For instance, fishermen usually worship in temples dedicated to Tin Hau, the guardian of seamen. Sometimes statues of Buddhist and Taoist gods, together with Confucian ancestral tablets, can be found in the same temple.

Folk religion is still strong and ancestor worship continues. When someone dies, his relatives usually burn all sorts of paper objects —representing houses, automobiles, money, and other luxuries that he might not have been able to afford in this world, but which he will enjoy in the next. A small shrine to the Taoist god, To Tei, can be found at the entrance to most homes and shops. Joss sticks, in groups of three, are always burned in front of the shrine.

In the New Territories, the homes of the living and the tombs of departed ancestors are located according to the principles of Fung Shui. Graves and houses must be in harmony with the natural surroundings, an example of the innate Chinese love of beauty. Fung Shui "experts" are often consulted, and they often demand large fees for their services.

EDUCATION

Scholarship has always been respected by the Chinese. Even in Imperial China a man of humble background could rise to a position of eminence in the government if he had sufficient intellectual capacity. In Hong Kong, education remains the key to advancement and success. At present about 75 per cent of the population is literate, 91 per cent of the men but only 58 per cent of the women. This reflects the desire of Chinese families to give their male offspring an education even if the family cannot afford to send all its children to school.

Because of the rapid population increase, the Hong Kong Government has undertaken a massive school-construction scheme. A new school opens every few weeks. Some schools are built by the Government; others are built with the aid of Government grants or loans. Education is not free in Hong Kong, but some places are reserved for children whose parents are unable to pay school fees.

Most primary schools use Cantonese as the medium of instruction, with English as a second language. However, the majority of secondary schools teach in English. These schools are very popular because a knowledge of English is essential for a University education and for positions in the Hong Kong Govern-

(Above) Each intricate Chinese character represents a word, and students must spend considerable time committing them to memory. Parents sometimes help their children with homework.

(Left) Private enterprise and Government money paid for Hong Kong's Technical College which provides trained personnel for the Colony's manufacturing industries. Girls in the commerce department are virtually assured of finding employment with local firms after they complete their courses.

(Right) Chinese schoolgirls hurry off to classes. The cheongsams *(slit skirts) they are wearing are part of their school uniform.*

(Left) Guiding school children across a street is a pleasant duty for this policeman. Children are taught to beware of traffic hazards from an early age; traffic is heavy, since the Colony has only a limited network of roads, and the number of vehicles using them increases yearly.

(Below) Every two weeks a new school opens in the race to keep up with the expanding population. Schools are often built in conjunction with new housing estates.

ment and business firms dealing in international commerce.

The University of Hong Kong is a leading institution of higher learning in the Far East. It was founded in 1911, and it is the only English-speaking, British-oriented University in this part of the world. Competition for entry is keen, and facilities are being expanded to keep up with the increasing population pressure. The University boasts faculties of Arts, Science, Medicine, Engineering and Architecture.

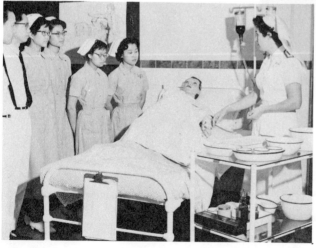

(Left) Hong Kong has a pressing need for hospital space. The Government, in co-operation with private groups, is expanding hospital facilities; nurses to staff the hospitals receive training in either English or Cantonese.

These police dogs performing at a fair in the New Territories are effective enemies of Hong Kong's criminal element. Westerners often have the impression that Hong Kong is a den of treachery and theft—a place where an innocent tourist is likely to be killed for his undershirt. Actually, statistics show that it is safer to live in Hong Kong than in New York City!

(Below) Basketball is as popular in Hong Kong as it is in the United States. Government-built community centers provide recreational and educational opportunities for people of all ages, and special clubs are run for the blind and the deaf.

SPORTS AND RECREATION

Even with the small, restricted area of the Colony, its residents manage to find room for an amazing variety of sports. Soccer is the most popular among both Chinese and Westerners. Teams from as far away as Peru and Switzerland often stop in Hong Kong to play against local teams. Surprisingly enough, local sides usually do quite well against foreign competition.

As could be expected, the British arrived in Hong Kong with cricket bats ready for play. They also brought golf, rugby, badminton and horse racing with them. The racing track is operated by the Royal Hong Kong Jockey Club, which turns over all profits to charity. In the past fifteen years the Club has donated many millions to community social welfare projects.

Basketball, an import from the United States, is very popular among the Chinese, and courts in public parks are constantly in use. Sea bathing and yachting are popular ways for cooling off in the hot summer sun.

A visitor walking down almost any one of Hong Kong's narrow, tenement-lined streets at any time of day or night is likely to hear the murmur of excited Chinese voices punctuated

Cheung Chau islanders pay their respects to the souls of fish and animals they have eaten during the year in a four-day bun festival. On the last day of the festival, villagers from the island storm the sides of 60-foot towers which are covered with thousands of delicious buns. Competition for the highest bun is especially keen.

by sharp clicking sounds. These noises come from Mah Jongg games. Mah Jongg, which is believed to have originated in China sometime during the 19th century resembles several Western card games in many ways, except that it is played with up to 144 domino-like tiles bearing Chinese characters. At Mah Jongg parties quite a lot of money often changes hands. During the 1920's a Mah Jongg fad swept the United States.

The actors and actresses in Chinese operas spend considerable time in applying heavy coats of make-up to their faces. The brilliantly-hued robes they wear are very costly.

(Below) Elaborate costumes, heavily-rouged faces, and clashing cymbals make Chinese opera a fascinating spectacle for foreign visitors in Hong Kong. The time-proven plots of most Chinese operas recount tales of love, war and intrigue.

THE ARTS

Hong Kong came into being for commercial reasons. Understandably, then, the Colony has not developed into a citadel of culture. It is especially weak in contributions from the West, although foreign musicians, ballets, and other artists often perform in the Colony during tours of the Far East. But the Chinese community has not been caught flatfooted. One of the most popular activities is the Chinese theatre, sometimes called Chinese opera. To a visitor, the most striking features of Chinese opera are noise and informality. The noise comes from a casually-clad orchestra playing traditional Chinese instruments. Sing-song voices of the actors and actresses are frequently punctuated by the clashing of cymbals and gongs. The audience behaves as if it were at a football game rather than a theatrical performance. People come and go, chat with their friends, and purchase snacks from roving food vendors.

The plays themselves are drawn from the rich storehouse of Chinese classics. There is no attempt to imitate reality. Actors wear the elaborate, many-splendored costumes of old China, while their faces are heavy with red make-up. The costumes reveal the character's

49

(Left) This seven-foot tusk once graced an African elephant. It will soon be carved into an assortment of chessmen, lampshades and other ivory items by skilled Chinese craftsmen. Examples of finished products can be seen in the display case.

(Above right) A craftsman chisels out a complicated design on what will soon be the lid of a red-wood chest.   Like most of his fellow wood carvers, he prefers to work squatting on the floor, rather than standing at a workbench.

(Right) Bridges carved from elephant tusks take up to 20 days to make, depending upon their size. The intricate detail of temples, bridges, people and trees represents Chinese paradise. Carvers must spend at least five years as apprentices before they are considered fully competent. Families sometimes pass on the skill from generation to generation.

50

Figurines representing characters from Chinese mythology are popular items. The figurine in the foreground is of Kwan Yin, eight-armed Goddess of Mercy.

social status and occupation, make-up indicates moral quality. For instance, all villains have red marks on their foreheads.

Hong Kong is a world leader in the production of motion pictures. Its huge output of over 300 feature films annually is distributed to theatres in Hong Kong, Taiwan, and other countries having Chinese populations. Most Hong Kong-made films are low-cost, low-quality productions, but a few usually win awards in the Asian Film Festival. Motion picture production is a good example of Chinese use of Western technology to popularize their own cultural heritage.

Chinese handicrafts need no introduction. Jade and ivory carving are probably the best-known crafts in Hong Kong. Prices for ivory carvings range from low sums for a simple figure to several thousands for exceptionally intricate and difficult works. Elephant tusks from Africa furnish the raw material for ivory carvers; often the entire tusk is used for a single carving. Ivory carving is not an occupation to be learned from a teach-yourself book. At least five years of apprenticeship is necessary for a carver to learn the demanding skills of the craft.

(Below) The steep mountainsides of Hong Kong often dictate its building styles. The modern Chinese Methodist Church in Kowloon makes maximum use of the valuable plot of land on which it is built.

(*Left*) *Women check the quality of newly-woven cloth. Western textile manufacturers, troubled by competition from Hong Kong imports, often conjure up spectres of thousands of exploited Chinese workers slaving away in dingy factories from dawn to dusk. This is not the case at all. The most successful textile factories in Hong Kong use modern equipment and provide their employees with comprehensive welfare benefits.*

(*Above*) *Many junk builders prefer to use traditional Chinese tools instead of their more modern Western counterparts. The shank of the drill is connected to the long bow by a cord, and when the boatmaker moves the bow back and forth, he activates the drill.*

(*Left*) *Chinese workers use Swiss and British machinery to mass-produce alarm clocks for customers in Iran, Mexico and other countries. Most of this firm's workers are women; they are paid according to the skill required for their particular job.*

Hong Kong is the last port of call for many venerable ships. Buyers from the Colony roam the ports of the world looking for ships being sold for scrap. These are brought to Hong Kong and cut up with acetylene torches. Local rolling mills turn the scrap steel into reinforcing rods and bars for use in the Colony, and for export to countries in Southeast Asia.

ECONOMY

Until about 1951, Hong Kong depended almost entirely upon the shipping trade and associated industries for its livelihood. The Harbour was the focus of the Colony's economic life. A few industries such as rope making, ship repairing, and sugar refining existed and grew in response to the demands of shipping.

Hong Kong staged a rapid recovery from the unfortunate years of Japanese occupation during World War II. The China trade increased and Hong Kong merchants discovered new markets in Southeast Asia. New trade records were set in 1950 and 1951. Then disaster struck.

In 1951 there began the Korean War between the United Nations—including Great Britain and the United States—on one side,

and North Korea, ably assisted and supplied by so-called Chinese Communist "volunteers," on the other side. To prevent valuable war supplies manufactured in the West from reaching the Communist side of the Korean battle lines, the Hong Kong Government banned the shipment of hundreds of "strategic" products to Communist China. The United States then declared an embargo on all trade with China, and, in view of Hong Kong's close trade relations with China, the embargo also included Hong Kong. The Colony suddenly found itself cut off from a major customer and source of raw materials for her few infant industries. As if these blows were not enough, China had another one in store for Hong Kong; the Communists began

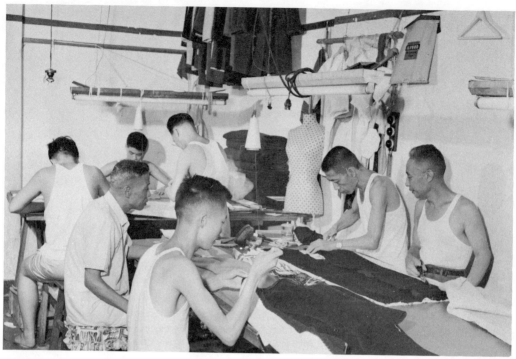

Need a new custom-tailored suit in 24 hours? Impossible, you might say. But in Hong Kong the impossible can—and does—happen! Industrious Chinese tailors are still hard at work long after Western tailors have quit for the day. The quality, of course, depends on the price you are willing to pay, but suits of the finest quality are far less expensive in Hong Kong than they are in New York or London.

(Below) Ships from all over the Far East and Australia are sent to Hong Kong's efficient dockyards for repair and overhaul. Here, workmen are repairing the bow of a dry-docked freighter. Boats ranging in size from pleasure craft to ocean-going vessels of 6,500 tons are built to order in the Colony.

making government-to-government barter trading arrangements with other countries. This effectively short-circuited the Colony's position as middleman in the China trade.

The future indeed looked grim for Hong Kong by the end of 1951. Unemployment was high and refugees continued to pour into the Colony. But the refugees proved to be the key to the future. A number brought large amounts of capital with them when they fled China, while others possessed a wide variety of technical skills. The hordes of refugee peasants that crowded into squatter villages and tenements represented a vast, untapped reservoir of unskilled and semi-skilled workers. At the same time, the United States eased its ban on trade with Hong Kong.

With these enticing ingredients at hand, no Chinese could afford to miss such a golden business opportunity. The Chinese seem to have a natural attraction to commerce and industry, and are often willing to take great risks in business ventures. It is small wonder then that within a decade Hong Kong became one of the Far East's leading manufacturing cities.

Today, Hong Kong's factories produce ever-increasing quantities of an enormous diversity of products. Woollen gloves, plastic chopsticks, clocks, cutlery, air-conditioners, tennis shoes,

Children all over the world play with dolls that were made in Hong Kong factories. This woman is sewing clothes for the dolls. While laws regulate the working hours of women, an eight-hour shift for all workers in the manufacturing industry, regardless of sex, is becoming widespread.

and scores of other types of manufactured goods bearing the imprint "Made in Hong Kong" are shipped to markets around the world. Hong Kong factories are of assorted sizes and shapes. At the top of the pyramid are

(Below) Workers from a factory at Kwun Tong head for lunch. A few years ago, the site of Kwun Tong was an inlet of Kowloon Bay; reclamation work here will ultimately create housing, factories, and shops for a city of 250,000.

(Above) Just point out the fabric and style you want, and a Hong Kong tailor will be glad to satisfy your request.

A Chinese girl, daughter of a New Territories farmer, leads the family's prize-winning water buffalo around the ring at an agricultural fair. Competition at such shows encourages improved agricultural methods among farmers.

the large, modern firms employing from several hundred to several thousand workers. Employees of these companies receive, by Hong Kong standards, high wages and a variety of fringe benefits, such as free medical care and subsidized housing. At the bottom of the pyramid are hundreds of small firms existing under marginal circumstances. For example, a flashlight "factory" or an "assembly plant" actually consists of a family and group of friends working in such an unlikely place as a squatter shack. Machinery is often ancient and decrepit, with little more than baling wire and twine holding it together. The industrious Chinese manage to locate their factories almost anywhere.

But success in industry has brought its share of problems, too. Hong Kong itself can absorb only a small fraction of the goods it produces. To survive, the Colony must export its manufactures. However, the sudden appearance of cheap, good quality Hong Kong merchandise in the stores and shops of Western nations has caused trade unions and management in these industrial countries to shudder. They fear unemployment and financial loss for themselves as a result of being undersold by cheaper products from Hong Kong. To protect themselves, they urge their own governments to restrict imports from Hong Kong by imposing high tariffs or quotas.

Hong Kong is attempting to solve this problem by negotiating agreements with the countries involved—the United States and Great Britain alone account for almost half of Hong Kong's total exports. The Colony is also engaged in an energetic search for new foreign markets. The long-range solution for Hong Kong is to diversify production further and improve the quality of its products, so that overseas customers will demand Hong Kong goods because of their high quality rather than their low price.

Soy sauce (used in almost all Chinese cooking) is manufactured in Hong Kong according to ancient recipes. Soya beans are imported from China and the United States and are then subjected to up to six months of delicate processing before the sauce is ready for sale. Here, soya beans are fermenting in Shanghai jars.

(Above) Melons prepared and canned under exacting hygienic conditions are exported to other countries. Hong Kong packers do a brisk business satisfying American and European appetites for bean sprouts, water chestnuts, lotus seeds, and other Chinese delicacies. (Below right) Farmers have built terraces along the fringes of the Shatin Valley in the New Territories to provide additional land for growing rice.

AGRICULTURE

Because of the mountainous terrain, only about 13 per cent of Hong Kong's land, mainly in the New Territories, is suitable for farming. But the agriculture on that small portion is intensive. Rice, the staple of Chinese diets, is the main crop. Because of the climate, two crops can be raised annually. The sight of Chinese farmers planting rice with their heads shielded from the strong sun by broad-brimmed straw hats is a familiar one in the New Territories. The ungainly-looking but useful water buffalo takes the place of a tractor for most farmers.

(Above) Two crops of rice are grown each year in the New Territories. The fields are first flooded; they are then churned into the proper consistency by a buffalo-drawn wooden plow. Women in the background are planting rice seedlings in the mud, by hand. The field in the foreground has just been planted and should be ready for harvesting in about 100 days.

A farmer is watering his small, carefully-tended vegetable plot with an effective home-made contrivance. Surplus vegetables will be sold in a market town. Delicious papayas will soon ripen on the white-trunked trees in the background.

FISHING

Not many years ago pirates sometimes attacked Hong Kong fishermen off the China coast. The pirates are gone, but the fishermen remain to exploit Hong Kong's largest natural resource. The waters in and around the Colony teem with a large variety of fish. More than 10,000 boats, mostly picturesque motorized or wind-powered Chinese junks, are engaged in fishing. It is a family occupation, and about 80,000 Chinese (known as the Tanka) spend most of their lives on board fishing junks.

A private, non-profit Fish Marketing Organization controls the sale of the catch. Fish are brought to central markets and auctioned to the highest bidder. The Organization also loans money to fishermen, so they can purchase modern equipment.

Sails are down and fish nets up to dry at this anchorage on Lantau Island. The shore is lined with straw baskets holding fish paste to be dried in the sun.

(Left) A batch of fry is being prepared for transfer to a fattening pond. The fish farmer in the foreground had better be wearing a waterproof watch or he may be in for an unpleasant surprise !

The fish mature in about a year; after that it's simply a matter of cruising around in a sampan and casting a net into the crowded pond. Most of the fish caught are sent to the city for sale.

The life of a fisherman is not easy. He must spend many long hours keeping his boat, nets and other equipment in good working order, besides the time he passes at sea, fishing.

Junks are not mass-produced but are still built in the manner they have been for centuries. The tools used are of ancient design and work progresses slowly, but a buyer can be certain he is purchasing a seaworthy ship.

No, the owners of this fishing junk haven't gone out of their minds! Heat from the rice-straw fire will burn the pitch between the hull timbers so that the vessel can be recaulked.

(Below) Tourists find Hong Kong a bargain mecca. Prices in Chinese shops are not fixed, and shoppers must be prepared to haggle over the price of an item for some time before the current market price is reached.

TOURISM

Catering to tourists from foreign countries has become a major industry and source of revenue for Hong Kong. In 1970, over 900,000 visitors from the United States, the British Commonwealth, and elsewhere come to sample life in the Colony. The flood of tourists has sparked a hotel construction boom which seems to be just about keeping up with the growing stream of sightseers and businessmen.

Hong Kong is a free port; no import duties are levied on practically all types of foreign merchandise. Swiss watches and Japanese cameras are therefore less expensive in the Colony than they are in Switzerland and Japan.

Tsuen Wan is a thriving industrial town built on reclaimed land in the New Territories. Started only a few years ago, Tsuen Wan will eventually be the home for 1,200,000 people and thousands of factories.

THE FUTURE

What the future holds in store for Hong Kong, no one is quite certain. Those in the best position to know are the rulers of Communist China. They are even more violent in their denunciations of Western colonialism than the Soviet Union is, yet they permit Hong Kong, a galling reminder of a century of Western imperialism, to exist on their very doorstep. If the communists in China really desired to seize Hong Kong, it is doubtful whether they would wait for the lease on the New Territories to expire on July 1, 1997. They possess the military might needed to wrest the Colony from Britain, but they would not even have to use force. For, by cutting off supplies of food, water, and raw materials, the Chinese Communists could starve the Colony into submission. Hong Kong's position is something like Berlin's, except that the loyalty of most West Berliners to the Western cause cannot be questioned, while that of Hong Kong's Chinese can at best be described as unknown.

Apparently, Communist China allows the Colony to remain because it is more valuable alive than dead. In fact, Hong Kong serves as China's window to the Western world, the way of life it so often bitterly attacks. Motion pictures, novels, and television shows depict Hong Kong as a seething den of international intrigue. This is only a partially correct description. There are spies and counterspies in Hong Kong, but they are also found in almost any country. Hong Kong is valuable to both Communist China and the West because it is a common ground for exchange of a vast amount of information of all sorts—the size of China's rice crop, new Government appointments, and Chinese progress on the atomic bomb to name but a few. Some of this information is ultra-secret, but a good deal of it is only as far away as the nearest library. In the hands of a trained intelligence expert who can separate fact from fiction such information can be extremely useful. It is safe to assume that all interested parties benefit from the exchange.

Communist China also finds Hong Kong important for another reason. The Colony is a good customer for Chinese merchandise. China receives payment in Western currencies. Thus, when China recently experienced a severe drought, it had available the hard cash necessary to pay for millions of bushels of Australian and Canadian wheat. A good part of this money probably came from trade with Hong Kong. The mingling of economic interests between capitalists and Communists shows itself in many fascinating ways in Hong Kong. For example, the offices of the famous British-owned Hong Kong and Shanghai Banking Corporation, which formerly financed much of the British commercial activity within China, are next door to the offices of the Communist-owned Bank of China.

In any event, the Communist disturbances of 1967, far from inhibiting economic growth, seem to have strengthened the will to survive in the Colony. The factor most likely to slow development at present is a shortage of technicians needed in new industries, to produce better quality products. If technical training facilities are not greatly expanded, Hong Kong stands to lose markets to Singapore, Taiwan and South Korea.

Freight cars ride across the railway bridge at Lowu, but train passengers walk. Hong Kong's boundary with Communist China is at the far end of the bridge; the Chinese flag and a red star can be seen just beyond it. Western businessmen, missionaries and soldiers held captive by the Chinese Communists are occasionally given their freedom at the Lowu bridge, an event which always attracts an interested group of journalists and news photographers.